# STEVEN UNIVERSE ™

## A CARTOON NETWORK ORIGINAL

created by
**REBECCA SUGAR**

written by
**GRACE KRAFT**

chapters five and seven
illustrated by
**MEG OMAC**

chapter six
illustrated by
**RII ABREGO**

chapter eight
written by
**MELANIE GILLMAN**

illustrated by
**KATY FARINA**

colours by
**WHITNEY COGAR**

letters by
**MIKE FIORENTINO**

cover by
**MISSY PEÑA**

Special Thanks to
Marisa Marionakis, Janet No, Curtis Lelash, Conrad
Montgomery, Jackie Buscarino, Alan Pasman
and the wonderful folks at Cartoon Network.

# CHAPTER FIVE

WOOOO!

L'WOOOOOO

SKIDDDD

WOW! THAT WENT SURPRISINGLY WELL!

LUCKY FOR US IT WAS A PRETTY SMALL GEM BEAST.

THAT WAS SO COOL HOW YOU CAUGHT IT OFF-GUARD WITH YOUR SWORD.

YOU'VE REALLY BEEN PRACTICING HUH?

YEAH! I HAVE!

BUT WE WOULD HAVE BEEN IN A PINCH IF IT WASN'T FOR YOUR SHIELD.

AW SHUCKS!

PAP PAP

HEY, WHERE DID LION WANDER OFF TO?

POFF

WELL, I CAN SEE YOU TWO ARE GETTING ALONG WELL.

I'LL JUST LEAVE YOU TWO TO YOUR PLAYDATE.

*UGH!* THAT'S IT!!

I DON'T WANT MY HAIR FULL OF LION SLOBBER.

I DON'T KNOW AMETHYST, I THINK IT'S A GOOD LOOK FOR YOU.

OH HUSH MISS NEVER-HAS-A-HAIR-OUT-OF-PLACE.

HAHA SORRY BIG GUY, IT'S JUST ME.

AND HOW DID YOU FIND MY SWORD COLLECTION? UGH! WHAT A MESS!

YOU'VE CAUSED ENOUGH TROUBLE HERE, NOW SHOO! GO ON!

STARE

W-WHAT? NO, YOU'RE SUPPOSED TO LEAVE!

THESE SWORDS AREN'T YOUR PLAYTHINGS.

BAP BAP

OH, WHATEVER...

SWIPE!

NOW SHOO ALREADY!

MRRR...

SNFF
SNFF

BIG
DONUT

EAT A
BIG
Donut

SMOOSH

OH, YOU REALLY LIKE THESE HUH?

LION LICKERS

*PUFF*

WELL I'VE SEEN STEVEN GIVE THESE TO YOU SO I GUESS IT'S OKAY.

I'LL GIVE YOU ONE, MY TREAT.

OH!

SHAKE SHAKE

THANKS FOR STOPPING BY!

GRAOOOH!

*SNORT* HAHA WOW

THIS IS A GOOD LOOK FOR YOU PERIDOT. PERIDOT...?

SPLOSHH!

GAH!

OH! IS THAT LION?

GUESS WE WERE RIGHT, HE DID JUST KEEP SLEEPING WHILE WE WERE AWAY.

MUST BE NICE BEING ABLE TO JUST TAKE IT EASY FOR A BIT.

OR MAYBE THAT'S JUST WHAT HE WANTS US TO THINK!

MAYBE HE WENT ON ALL SORTS OF ADVENTURES JUST TO WIND UP BACK HERE IN TIME FOR US TO SUSPECT NOTHING.

*GASP* JUST LIKE THOSE PETS ON TV THAT LIVE DOUBLE LIVES!

HAHAHAHA!

HAHA, WOULDN'T THAT BE SOMETHING?

YEAH, C'MON! WE GOTTA HURRY IF WE'RE GOING TO CATCH THE LATEST EPISODE OF CRYING BREAKFAST FRIENDS!

END

# CHAPTER SIX

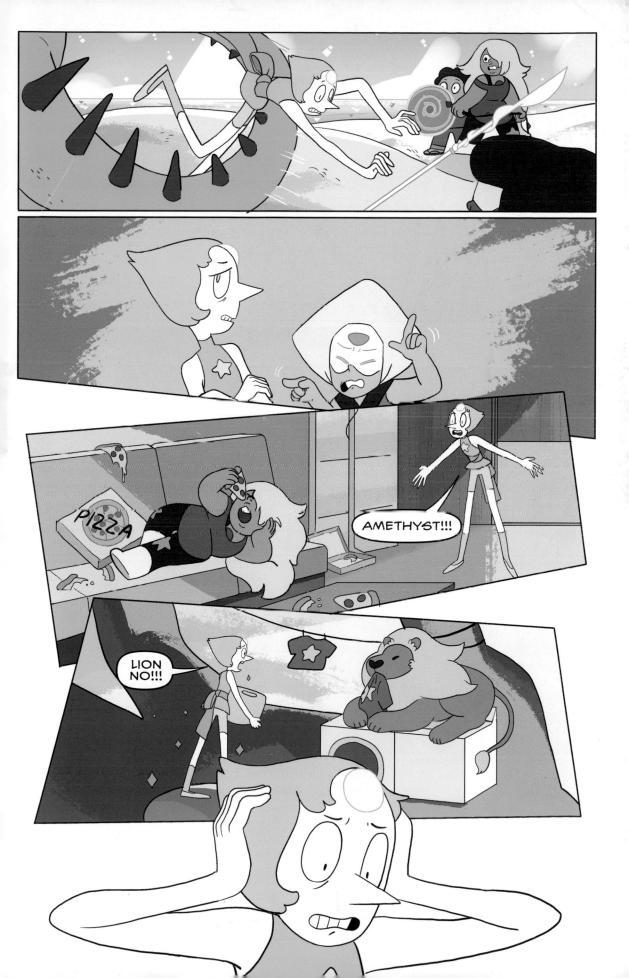

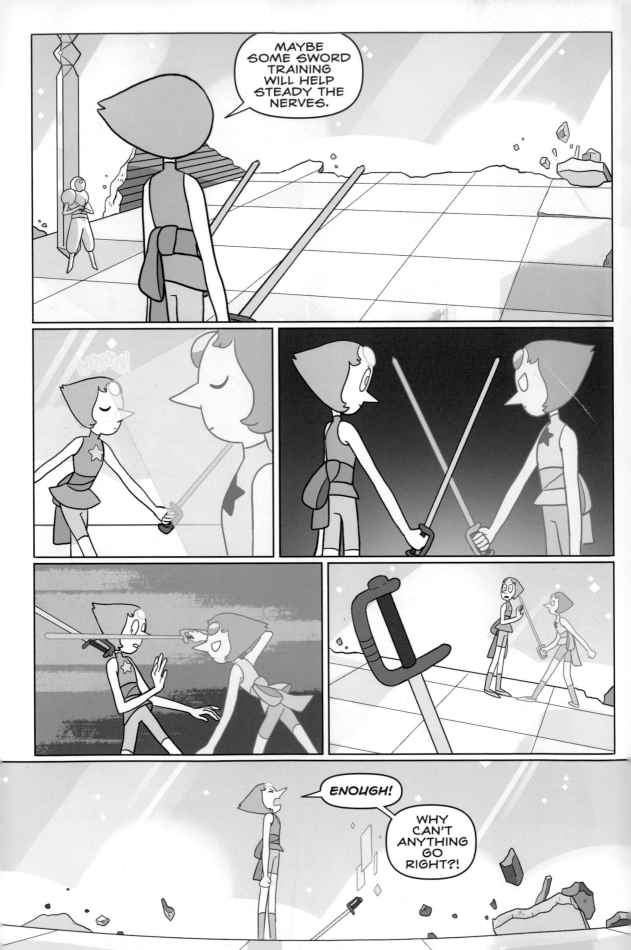

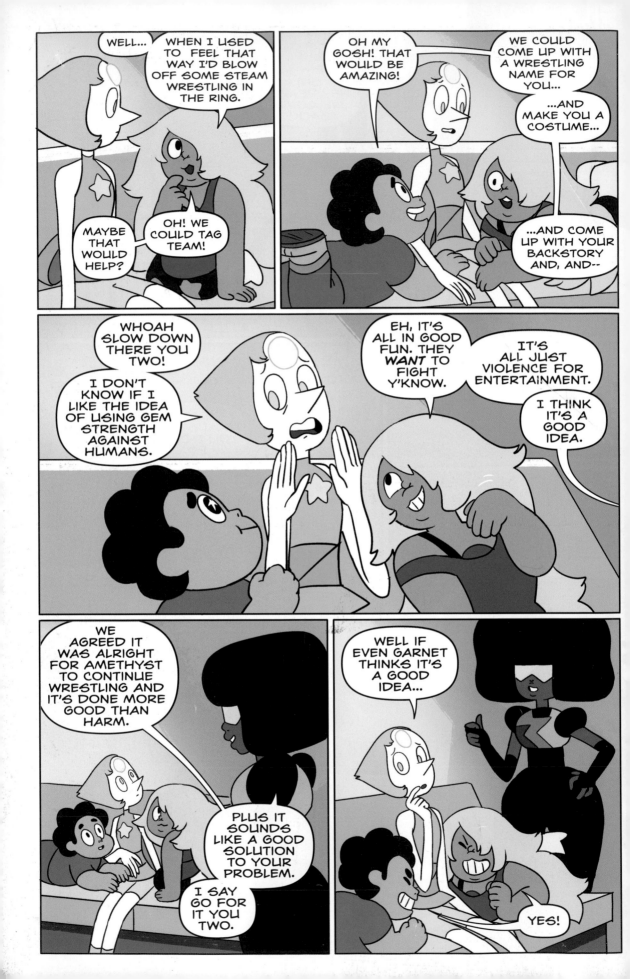

NOW WE JUST NEED TO FIGURE OUT YOUR COSTUME.

COSTUME? SHOULDN'T I JUST BE WEARING THE APPROPRIATE WRESTLING ATTIRE?

WELL, PART OF WRESTLING IS ALSO ABOUT MAKING A CHARACTER THAT THE AUDIENCE CAN GET INVESTED IN.

AND PART OF THAT IS COSTUME.

I WORE THIS TIGER MASK WHEN I WRESTLED AS TIGER MILLIONAIRE.

MAYBE YOU COULD USE IT TOO?

BAHAHAHA!

OKAY MAYBE NOT THOSE.

I THINK I'VE GOT SOME PINK CAT EARS UNDER HERE.

I DON'T KNOW STEVEN...

PLEEEAASE?

HAHA, OH ALRIGHT.

LADIES AND GENTLEFOLKS!

ALL FANS OF WRESTLING!

TONIGHT DO WE HAVE A REAL TREAT FOR YOU!

IN THE RING, WE HAVE A SURPRISE, ONE-NIGHT RETURN OF OUR OLD FAVORITE VILLAINOUS WRESTLER TO BOO!

PURPLE PUMA!

BUT JOINING HIM IN THE RING TONIGHT IS A NEW PARTNER!

A LONG-TIME FRIEND OF PUMA, OUR NEW CONTENDER OFTEN FOUGHT AND BUTTED HEADS WITH PUMA.

BUT NOW THEY ARE PLAYING ON THE SAME TEAM!

GIVE IT UP FOLKS, FOR THE PEACH PANTHER!

AND HERE COME THEIR FIRST CHALLENGERS OF THE EVENING, THE WOLVES OF WALL STREET!

RAAAAAH!

...AND THAT'S WHY RIGHT NOW IS A GREAT TIME TO INVEST IN STOCKS FOR EMPIRE CITY TECHNOLOGIES.

AND...WHY DO I WANT TO DO THIS AGAIN?

OH! AND WITH THAT PURPLE PUMA AND PEACH PANTHER CLAIM THEIR FIRST VICTIMS TO THEIR TAG TEAM ONSLAUGHT!

WHAM!

PAN-THER WHAT WAS THAT?!

YOU CAN'T JUST STAND THERE AND TALK TO THE GUY!

WE'RE HERE TO FIGHT!

HEY! DON'T YELL AT ME! I'M STILL NEW TO THIS!

UGH SORRY, I JUST GET REALLY INTO IT WHEN I GET IN THE RING.

ALRIGHT, LOOK.

REMEMBER THAT FRUSTRATION YOU WERE TELLING ALL OF US ABOUT EARLIER?

YES?

WELL, USE IT TO GET ANGRY AND FIRED UP AND READY TO FIGHT AND STUFF!

AND NOW, ENTERING THE RING WE HAVE THE BROTHERS CONSTRUCTION!

NOW, YOU SEE THAT GUY?

PRETEND HE'S ALL THOSE THINGS THAT MADE YOU MAD.

AND JUST LET HIM HAVE IT!

LET HIM HAVE WHAT?

YOU KNOW! A TASTE OF YOUR FURY!

AND CHUNK TRUCK HAS PEACH PANTHER PINNED DOWN TO THE MAT!

PANTHER HAS UNTIL THE COUNT OF THREE TO GET BACK UP ON HER FEET.

C'MON PEAR--I MEAN PANTHER! YOU CAN TAKE THIS GUY EASILY!

OH WHAT'S THE USE, I CAN'T GET THE HANG OF THIS. DECIDING TO DO THIS WAS A MISTAKE.

MAYBE I SHOULD JUST ADD THIS DEFEAT TO THE REST OF MY GROWING COLLECTION.

ONE!

WHAT?!

THE GEM I KNOW DOESN'T QUIT THAT EASILY!

AREN'T YOU TIRED OF LETTING EVERYTHING HAPPENING LATELY KICK YOU AROUND?

FIGHT BACK!

TWO!

C'MON PEACH PANTHER! GET UP!

HRRGH!

HUH?

WOW FOLKS! WHAT A COME BACK!

PEACH PANTHER HAS SENT CHUNK TRUCK FLYING OUT OF THE RING!

HYAAAAAH!

WHOOOAAAH!

AAAAH!!

WOO! GO PEACH PANTHER!

OH, THANKS.

NO PROBLEM.

WOW! AN INCREDIBLE LAST-MINUTE DODGE BY PEACH PANTHER!

FWIP

BAM!

BUT PEACH PANTHER ISN'T OUT OF THE WOODS YET AS DASHING DANNY DOOBER CHARGES AFTER HER!

AND PEACH PANTHER DELIVERS A POWERFUL LEG SWEEP KNOCKING DANNY RIGHT OFF OF HIS FEET!

SWIPE!

THIS LOOKS LIKE THIS COULD BE IT FOR DASHING DANNY DOOBER...

HANDSOME HANK HACKLESCHMIDT ATTEMPTS TO TAKE PEACH PANTHER BY SURPRISE BUT PURPLE PUMA IS NOT HAVING IT!

THANKS AM--ER PUMA!

HAHA NO WORRIES, I GOT YOUR BACK PANTHER!

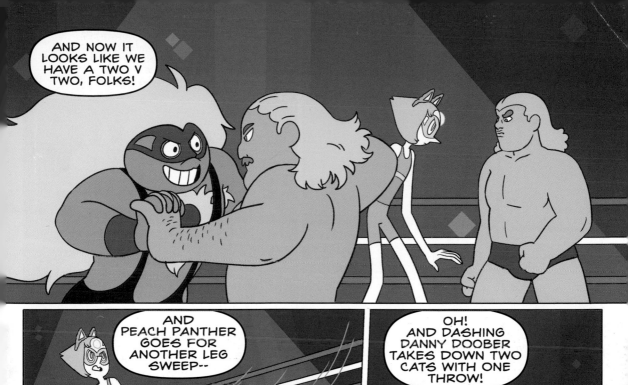

AND NOW IT LOOKS LIKE WE HAVE A TWO V TWO, FOLKS!

AND PEACH PANTHER GOES FOR ANOTHER LEG SWEEP--

--BUT DASHING DANNY DOOBER CATCHES IT THIS TIME!

CATCH!

OH! AND DASHING DANNY DOOBER TAKES DOWN TWO CATS WITH ONE THROW!

THE PUMA PANTHER DUO GOES DOWN AND THEY ARE NOT LOOKING TOO GOOD FOLKS!

COME ON, GET UP PUMA!

AREN'T YOU ALWAYS GOING ON ABOUT HOW SCRAPPY YOU ARE?

HAHA WOW P, YOU'RE REALLY INVESTED IN THIS NOW HUH?

OF COURSE I AM! WE CAN'T LET THEM WIN!

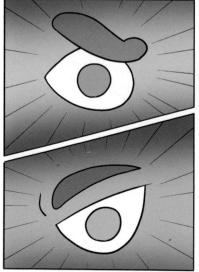

AND IT LOOKS LIKE THE GANG IS READYING THEIR OWN FINAL ATTACK!

THE GOOD-LOOKING GANG MAKES THEIR MOVE WHILE PUMA AND PANTHER ARE UNABLE TO RECOVER FAST ENOUGH!

SLAM-A-POW!

DING DING

AND IT LOOKS LIKE WE HAVE OUR WINNERS!

GIVE IT UP FOR THE GOOD-LOOKING GANG!

WOO! YAAAAAY!

HA HA HA HA!

OOF... I'M GOING TO FEEL THAT IN THE MORNING.

THOSE WRESTLERS ARE CERTAINLY ROUGH.

YEAH, BUT DON'T YOU FEEL BETTER?

I MEAN, YOU HAD FUN RIGHT? "PANTHER?"

YES, WE CERTAINLY DID...

"PUMA."

HAHAHA!

YOU BOTH DID GREAT.

YEAH! YOU GUYS WERE ALL LIKE... WHAM! RAM! KABLAM!

AND THOSE COMBO MOVES WERE AMAZING!

YOU TWO SHOULD TAG TEAM WRESTLE AGAIN!

WHY DON'T WE SAVE THOSE MOVES TO USE ON OUR NEXT MISSION INSTEAD?

HAHA! SOUNDS LIKE A PLAN!

END

# CHAPTER SEVEN

THANK YOU SO MUCH ONION!

SO WHAT ARE YOU UP TO TODAY WITH ALL THIS GEAR?

OH! ARE YOU GOING ON A FISHING TRIP WITH YOUR DAD?

THAT'S SO COOL!

I HOPE YOU GUYS HAVE A FUN TIME!

HERE, LET ME HELP YOU WITH YOUR STUFF.

HUH!

FISHERMAN GAL BEARS A STRIKING RESEMBLANCE TO ONION'S DAD.

NOW I KINDA WANT TO GO FISHING TOO...

OH MY GOSH! IS THAT THE GEM SLOOP?

I HAVEN'T SEEN YOU GUYS USE IT IN A LONG TIME...

HAHA YEP, IT'S THE OL' SLOOP.

WE NEED IT FOR A MISSION TODAY.

I PINPOINTED THE LOCATION OF A GEM ARTIFACT.

BUT IT'S OUT ON THE OCEAN FAR AWAY FROM ANY OTHER WARP PADS.

THAT'S SO COOL!

HOW MUCH LONGER UNTIL WE GET THERE?

MMM... IT'S STILL GOING TO BE A WHILE.

WELL IN THAT CASE, I'M GONNA DO A LITTLE FISHING!

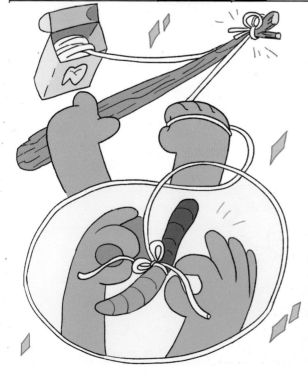

PLOOP!

THRASH!!

FLING!

CRASH

AAHH!!!

SPLOOSH!!

BOBBLE BOB

OH NO!

MY GUMMY WORMS...

HUH?

SNARF!

OH, I GUESS MY GUMMY WORMS ATTRACTED THE GEM BEAST OVER HERE.

I'M SORRY GUYS...

IT'S ALRIGHT, YOU COULDN'T HAVE KNOWN.

YEAH, I MEAN WHO WOULD'VE THUNK?

WELL, I KIND OF SAW IT COMING.

BUT IT SEEMED PRETTY UNLIKELY.

SO WHAT'S THE PLAN, G?

HMMM...

OH! IS THAT A BOAT?

MRRR MUHMUH!

SCHFFFF

POFF!

OH! THE GEM!

GOT IT!

BUT WHAT ABOUT THE--

*SIGH*

I'LL GET IT.

NOW THIS IS THE KIND OF FISHING I CAN HANDLE.

I THINK THAT'S EVERY LAST PIECE, P.

IT'S GOING TO BE A PAIN TO FIX IT BUT... IT WON'T BE IMPOSSIBLE.

I FOUND YOUR BAG IN THE SLOOP WRECKAGE!

SORRY IT GOT ALL SOGGY.

THANKS AMETHYST!

GARNET'S BACK!

SPLSH

MISSION COMPLETE, FINALLY.

WELL THAT WAS CERTAINLY AN... ORDEAL.

YEAH BUT AT LEAST WE'RE ALL DONE NOW.

AND WE GOT A GEM BEAST TO BOOT!

GOOD WORK, TEAM!

AND NOW WE HAVE TIME FOR A LITTLE FISHING!

OH! I THINK I'VE GOT A BITE!

**THE END**

# CHAPTER EIGHT

I WON!

AHHHHHH.

GUESS I'LL JUST WAIT FOR THE OTHERS TO CATCH UP.

EXIT

OH-GUESS I WASN'T THE ONLY ONE WHO SOLVED IT!

WELL KID, YOU DID GOOD, BUT YOU GOTTA BE FASTER THAN *THAT* TO BEAT *STEVEN QUARTZ UNIVERSE*--!

WHAT??

WHOA!!

I...DON'T THINK I SAW THIS ON THE MAZE MAP?

THIS SURE WOULD BE A GREAT TIME FOR GARNET'S FUTURE VISION TO TELL HER SHE SHOULDN'T HAVE LISTENED TO ME WHEN I SAID NOT TO USE FUTURE VISION!!

OKAY, LITTLE BUDDY-- HOLD ON, I'M COMING.

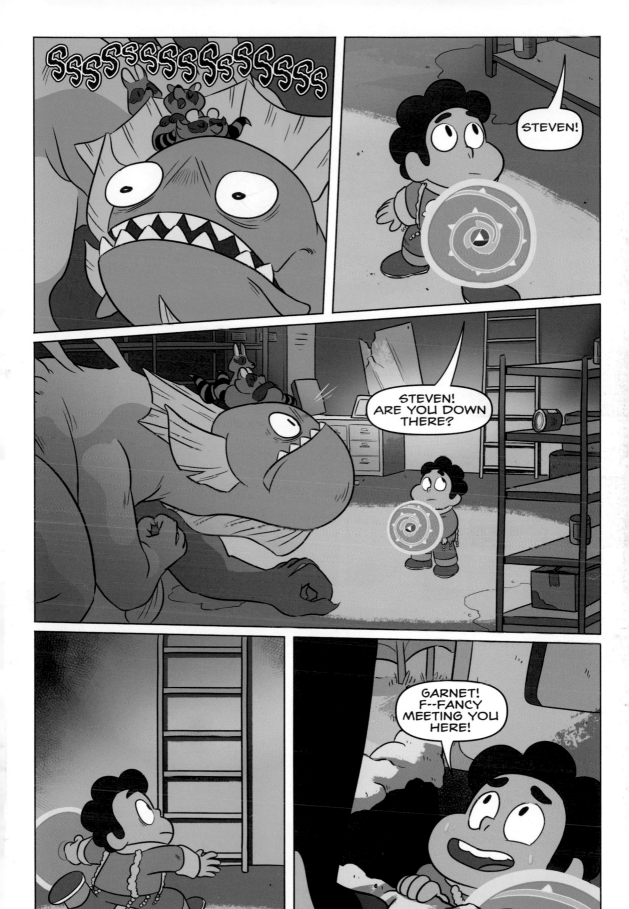

I FOUND THIS COOL HOLE IN THE GROUND, BUT THERE'S DEFINITELY NOTHING AT ALL IN IT!

ESPECIALLY NOT ANY, UH--

--MONSTERS.

...YEAH, THAT WAS NEVER GONNA WORK.

OKAY, MAYBE THERE IS ONE GEM MONSTER, BUT WE SHOULD LEAVE HER ALONE!

I THINK SHE HAS BABIES! AND SHE ONLY HISSED AT ME A LITTLE!

STEVEN, I APPRECIATE THAT YOU CARE SO MUCH. AND YOU ARE A VERY CUTE JELLYFISH.

BUT AS LONG AS THIS MAZE IS OPEN, HUMANS WILL BE COMING THROUGH HERE, TOO.

IF WE LEFT THE MONSTER ALONE, ARE YOU CERTAIN THE HUMANS WOULD ALL BE SAFE, TOO?

WAIT, I'VE GOT IT!

WE'LL JUST *REROUTE* THE HUMANS!

I CAN BLOCK THE ENTRANCE OVER HERE, AND YOU CAN PUNCH A NEW PATH TO THE EXIT OVER THERE!

Sssssssssssss

WAIT, GARNET!

AAAAAHH!!

OOF!

WAIT!!

OH NO....

NEXT TIME, MAYBE GIVE A GUY SOME WARNING BEFORE YOU PUNCH A MONSTER RIGHT NEXT TO HIS FACE??

YOU'RE WELCOME.

STEVEN-- THE BABIES WILL BE ALL RIGHT. TRUST ME.

I HOPE SO.

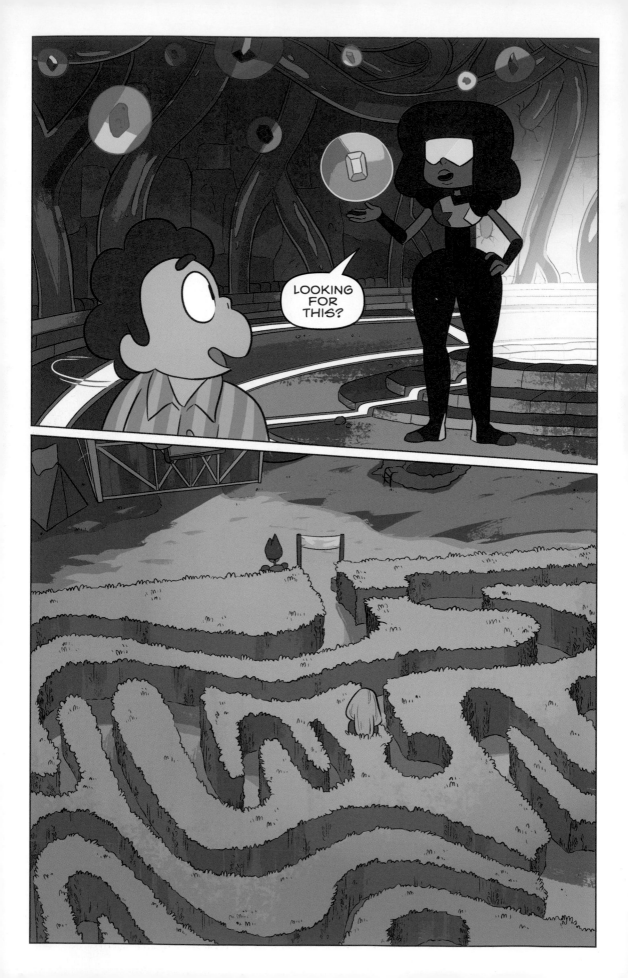

READY?

DO IT.

SORRY ABOUT THAT, FRIEND.

issue five main cover
**MISSY PEÑA**

issue five subscription cover
RIAN SYGH

issue five san diego comic-con exclusive cover
**PAULINA GANUCHEAU**

issue six variant cover
**SARA TALMADGE**

issue seven main cover

**MISSY PEÑA**

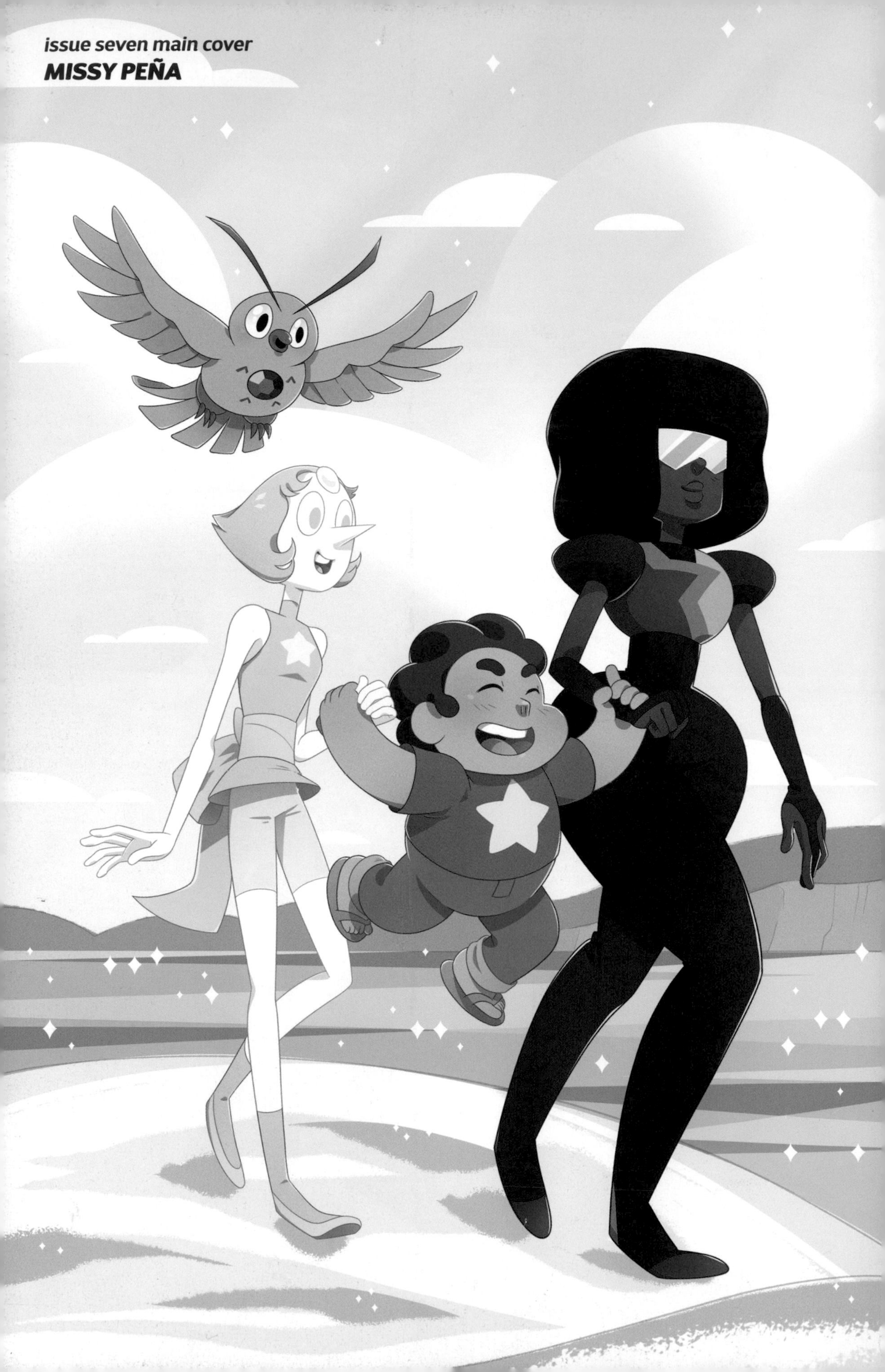

issue seven subscription cover
**JOSCELINE FENTON**

issue eight main cover
**MISSY PEÑA**